MW01002713

CALAMITIES

RENEE GLADMAN

WAVE BOOKS

SEATTLE / NEW YORK

Published by Wave Books

www.wavepoetry.com

Copyright © 2016 by Renee Gladman

Wave Books titles are distributed to the trade by

Consortium Book Sales and Distribution

Phone: 800-283-3572 / SAN 631-760X

Library of Congress Cataloging-in-Publication Data

Names: Gladman, Renee, author.

Title: Calamities / Renee Gladman.

Description: First edition. | Seattle ; New York : Wave Books, [2016]

Identifiers: LCCN 2015044539 | ISBN 9781940696287 (limited edition hardcover)

| ISBN 9781940696270 (softcover)

Classification: LCC PS3557.L2916 A6 2016 | DDC 813/.54—dc23

LC record available at http://lccn.loc.gov/2015044539

Designed and composed by Quemadura

Printed in the United States of America

9 8 7 6 5 4 3

Wave Books 057

CALAMITIES

I began the day with a group of characters, who were sometimes people in the world with real names and jobs that let them out for the summer; some of these characters wrote books in which the world was never mentioned, the world where one took a bus or walked through snow to buy eggs; it seemed better that the reader not know the details. I read in a book about a girl holding a stack of paper over a body of water; I read a book where a flood comes and covers a town, and though everything is wet all the people are dry; I read many books about people sitting in rooms, and these were all by writers I knew. I wanted them to come over, but they lived everywhere, in too many places. I wanted coffee when I had given it up; I wanted gluten all the time. At some point I began working on the beginning and end of something at once. I hadn't had my bases covered in a long time. I was reading a line in a book, then reading a line in another book, and performing small acts in between: I sat at intervals on the toilet, I slept sporadically, I ate kale and "fish food," and called myself "Renee" for a time. Nobody knew who I was at the grocery store, but going there was my big event. I knew the books of these people; I knew these people and I didn't change their names, but when they appeared in my books it wasn't really their stories I was telling, so they didn't need my protection and I could go "Danielle, Danielle" all day. I could say, "Danielle," and not disturb the Danielle who was sitting next to me, reading *Animal Architects*; because I could be saying "Danielle had had a certain body" or "Danielle was swishing across the floor," and the Danielle sitting next to me would go on reading her book. I could say "Lisa," who had written a book I loved, but also mean "Barbara," who *too* had written a book I loved, but say "Lisa" because of a sound I wanted to make, or simply to be anachronistic. I went on to fill my days with as many writers as I could find and sometimes would try to say their names or the names of their books or just the names of the cities they were in or just the name of a color or object I associated with them, though it wasn't their story I was telling. Because it wasn't their story, sometimes I just paused in my thinking and let them pass through me, and wouldn't resume until they were gone, or would resume when a trace of them was still there.

I began the day giving a lecture to a group of university students. I said, "—" and made a certain gesture with my hand. They asked, "How do you know," with some small showing of contempt. Well, I was trying to say, "It's okay to think," but maybe what they heard was "You don't think" or "You are not thinking." I made the "Let's start again" gesture with my eyebrows, and calm was restored. I started over from the top, "In any case, one can see the city—" I was interrupted before I could replace the errant word. These were conservative students. "I *mean*, the sentence!" I yelled over their clamor. And as they grew quiet, one of them muttered, "You don't think," but he hadn't planned on being heard. He said, "I think you don't think?" by way of correction. We were trying to get to the heart of the matter. I said, from the head of the class, "This is really good," and smiled grandly, with so much love falling from my cheeks I worried that Alex Peters, sitting in the front row, might explode with grief. Everyone else grew sad, too. But, we were approaching something that was perhaps new for all of us. Someone raised her hand. I don't remember who. She said, "We might not like your questions," but said it while smiling with her arm still up. I had to go on with my lecture: "When you turn in your mind, you reach somewhere, open something, make some gesture." I paused. My notes had quotes around them. I was almost done.

I began the day having given myself the task of compiling a list. I wanted to see whether I could trace all the problems—large and small—I had taken on in my somewhat long career as a writer. But I didn't mean those asinine problems of writer's block or other equally frustrating problems of self-worth (feeling too much or not enough). Rather, I wanted to document the questions that *led* to writing, writing such as I was doing then. I had to put my pen down. Suddenly, I was flooded with sensations of a sexual nature. I didn't know from where they'd come. As I just said, my mind was, in that moment, fixed on academic matters—what it meant to write and what I in fact had written—and usually I approached such topics with discipline: I was a serious writer; there was nothing inherently sensual in the act of writing (hands tapping at keys). So when out of nowhere I felt her pressing against my back I had to put my pen down. "What are you doing?" I asked an empty, flaming room.

I began the day thinking that in order to write a talk on "The Ongoing Story" I would need to incorporate it into these essays I'd been writing about my life. I began, "I began the day staring into the face of the question of narrative—was anybody still interested in it, and, if so, why?" It was a simple question to ask but had taken me eight days to write—you'd think it impossible to construct a sentence two words at a time, writing two words then taking the rest of the day off then on the next day writing two more words, maintaining the thread the whole time, until finally, on the eighth day, you had it, the sentence, but this sometimes happened when you were writing about narrative inside of narrative. Recently, I had found that to talk about something that was in essence everything was too exhausting, and that the only way around it was to talk about the question of the thing rather than the thing itself, since in the end, it would become both. "Narrative—" I went on with my talk, "Was anybody still interested? I didn't want to open my eyes to it. I hadn't wanted to think about narrative at the same time that I was conscious of my body lying in the object world. It was a problem of space similar to what Martha and I were discussing yesterday: Was it possible to say that something was gathering outside of a thing with the intention of meeting something else when this something else was the larger space in which that first thing existed? Could I talk about narrative as I was operating within it? I closed the quotes enclosing the text for my talk and took a train to New York. I wanted to surround myself with other people who were thinking about narrative and asking themselves whether they were for or against it. Someone was having an event that evening, and it seemed appropriate to the essay that I narrate the events of the event before they actually happened. But not for the essay inside which I was writing the panel talk, rather the outer essay in which I felt isolated and needed to travel three point five hours to be among people. When I opened the quotes again for the talk I was thinking, It wasn't just narrative we were talking about but narrative in relation to poetic time, which was not the time of the object world in which I was lying but *was* the time of the essay toward which I was attempting to *draw* the object world. Once the object world arrived I hadn't figured out what I would do in it (though you see the complication I was unearthing since I was already in it, the object world). This returned me to a conversation I was having elsewhere. I'd been arguing that the problem of poetic time was a component of fiction but now I saw: fiction could not concern itself with problems of time. If there was a problem inside a fiction—a problem of any nature other than what's happening inside the plot—then the whole thing would swell and small holes would form across the surface and the swellings would become as large as mountains while the holes would fill with water and become river valleys and soon we would be so far from the surface of the water that we'd recognize the picture of the mountains and valleys as part of a geological map and recognize ourselves standing in an object world much larger than the object world in which we'd been lying when we began this essay. I closed the quotes when I bottomed out. I would have to open my eyes if I wished to understand fully where I was and whom I was with, if anybody. The figures forming in the light directed toward my closed lids (by the sun or the lamp I'd failed to turn off before falling asleep the previous night or by the panel talk that I was living rather than writing) would not grow in definition so long as I carried on not-seeing in this way, I thought as I closed the quote on *this* narrative. I didn't want, in the middle of the whole thing, to become *anti-narrative*. After the event in New York, which was formulated around the celebration of the appearance of a long-awaited thing, I was disappointed to find people more anti-narrative than narrative.

Someone took my number instead of giving me hers—this was anti-narrative. We spent hours at a restaurant called the Half King and were given the wrong check, which, when corrected, turned out cheaper than the right check. This was anti-narrative. Those of us standing around the table, hoping there would be enough money to cover the bill, were thinking anti-narratively about the people who had evaded this torture by departing early, their contribution left behind. When we found there was enough money, even extra, we thought anti-narratively about our previous anti-narrative attack on those others. I wanted to turn our living toward narrative so suggested we all take the subway home. This was not agreed on, but we did all walk off together. Somehow it was only the black people who'd been in attendance that remained in our group. We walked along 23rd Street and I called a person and counted off the number of black people with me. I counted seven, narratively. This was astounding, but I didn't tell the other black people what I was thinking, only that person. This was anti-narrative. But clearly I was happy, as this configuration of blackness did not occur for me in the lonely little white city that I'd fled, thus was narrative. But within that, an anti-narrative moment, when I had to remind myself that it wasn't the little city that was white but rather the neighborhood in which I'd chosen to live. Imagine my surprise when I found it was possible to be both narrative and anti-narrative at the same time, which was like being a little overwhelmed in a large crowd. I was again pointed to a problem of time, or rather, space in time (it was hard to figure). How would I escape this crowd, but just to get outside it? Would it be possible to leave my name with someone? I closed the inner essay to look at the outer. I wanted to find a word or sentence that would prove there was an even larger essay that was further outside of this one. I closed the quotes of lying in the bed with my eyes closed, and opened my eyes, looking literally into the face of the question of narrative, which was the emptiness of my apartment and the long stretch of day that lay ahead.

I began the day having just uttered the words, "I am not looning up on claw," and feeling angry as a result of my disposition. It was as if I knew indisputably that I would never loon up "on claw" or any other substance that would threaten whatever in that dream was the opposite of *looning up*—I knew this, but it seemed I had to make my stance clear anyway. I was angry and thought I should go strictly decaf that morning, which had to be retrieved from the depths of the cabinet. It had been a week of procuring beans from all the continents, minus that very small one. It wasn't long before I realized I'd somehow looned up on decaf, though decaf was designed expressly to avoid such a thing. How confusing to have found yourself shaking as you brought a large mug of decaf to your lips. How ridiculous.

I began the day in a faculty meeting—though I was late in coming, having just walked into the room. I didn't know how I had gotten there. The doors were closed—that's how I knew I was late—and, much worse, locked when quietly I tried to open them. However, upon knocking, I heard the director say my name, and I thought at least I had been expected. A senior member opened the door and thought it would be a good time to play a joke on me, saying you can't come in here, though I'd just heard my name. I didn't think it was funny, since often I can't attend meetings, since being junior often meant I couldn't. But everyone laughed and welcomed me seniorly. Faculty meetings are strange; there is always someone there whose rank you don't understand, someone who had seemed just a visiting lecturer or scholar now sitting with his back very straight and holding a clipboard. Yes, in fact, it did seem that certain people in the room had been in a meeting before this one, a pre-meeting meeting as it were, and this newly important person had been among those in attendance. Some people were eating coffee cake. Some people were deaf and couldn't wait to leave the room, to return to the vibrations of their music. Some people were in town just for the day, eager to get on the next plane. Some people weren't there and soon became the topic of conversation. Some people were saying they were always there though this was clearly untrue to everyone in the room except those people. We didn't say anything, I think, because of the coffee cake, and suddenly the weather had grown beautiful, and we all felt it. But the agenda kept us sitting there and soon the sun was forgotten. We were talking about the thing that made me disagree with the majority of the room and this kept the clock ticking and got everyone full. You couldn't storm the halls in that manner, someone was saying, but you also couldn't forgive the infraction. I nestled into the corner. And the clipboard rang with paper. It was clear that some of us would go on wreaking havoc behind the scenes, and the director would write the memo. The meeting was over. We agreed that agreeing meant we could leave the room, so we agreed, and in some column this was important.

I began the day on an Amtrak train that was backing up. New England had flooded (once again) and become impassable: it had us pulling in then backing up then pulling forward then stopping and repeating these motions until, finally, we'd achieved the right alignment and passengers could disembark the train. This dusky place was New Haven and the platform was full of Connecticut commuters hurrying home in a light rain, in this month of May, which everyone expected to be hot in this part of the country, where what you had instead was a wet, perpetually cold feeling in the air. A voice came on. Apparently, the tracks had flooded. We needed to remain here. No, we needed to detrain and wait for buses in the station. No, the station was too crowded we should remain on the train. No, half in the station, half on the train. No, finally, it was decided: all on the train. My fellow passengers had grown tired and all tried to get into the café car at once. The voice came on again to say that the café car was closed. We were in a predicament. I hadn't moved. I hadn't become thirsty. There was some math to figure out: New England was becoming the Pacific Northwest. To be more specific, the Atlantic Northeast was becoming the Pacific Northwest, and quickly. First, I had to figure out what would happen to the Pacific Northwest once we had become it. It couldn't be that both northern ends of the opposite coasts would have twin weather systems. There was no place in logic for that. So if we were to become the Pacific Northwest, then the Pacific Northwest would have to undergo its own transformation. Obviously, the Pacific Northwest would not become the former Atlantic Northeast, because we could have just stayed what we were, if that were possible. No, it would be something more along the lines of declension, something being less than it was before, which was why I was doing math and not paying much attention to the conductor's voice, which was, if anything, loud and New England in nature. You had to understand the enormity of the problem. It would not be simply that the former Atlantic Northeast was now the Pacific Northwest, but that the environment—the people, how they called themselves, the structures they built—would have to change as well. You couldn't be the new Pacific Northwest and behave as if you were the former Atlantic Northeast, which technically you still were in terms of geography (though, soon, your new climate would make your landscape unrecognizable). So, what would happen to the New England personality? That was what I was trying to figure. It was not so good right now. It was tight, shut in, like winter but all year round. So, I was trying to understand what happened to a bad personality when the conditions in which it lived became worse, and couldn't help wondering why the former Atlantic Northeast wasn't always the new Pacific Northwest with the way people behaved. I mean, they really did already act as if all there was was rain.

I began the day asking the individuals of this group of my ex-lovers to map a problem of space, but not the problem that involved the anxiety of whether they could or could not draw, nor the one that asked how it was even possible to translate "problems" into lines, rather, I meant real problems, where you had to think about where you were in a defined space and what your purpose was for being there. We got thrown off course. One of our party was insisting that the "point" should be our vehicle of expression ("not the line") since it was the point that was the base of all communication. While I felt compelled to agree with her—the point certainly did take up less space than the line and seemed to be the originary gesture of all movement—I did have to counter that though the point may be the base of all communication, it could not function *as* the base, because most people did not begin looking at points until they became lines. We were having a picnic in the park, perched on a small hill, our bodies arranged on an old pink sheet from the 70s, decorated with a bloodred stripe. This was a time of the summer where Brooklyn had become a regular destination for me, and I was turning forty. I was turning forty so I felt that my ideas were very potent. Every time I found myself leaving an era at the same time that I was entering a new one, which was not always how it happened, sometimes something big ended and absolutely nothing followed it for a long, long time, except maybe you got fat or your sweet dog died, but on the occasion of going from thirty-nine to forty—well, it was one of those things where everyone filled in your sentences for you. You'd say something like, "I'm turning forty on Monday," and people, regardless of the degree of intimacy between you, began to tell you a story about themselves or a stranger or about *you* yourself—and yes, their stories did approximate some of what you'd been thinking over the past weeks, but why wouldn't they let you tell it? Impossible when it was a small picnic and you were among your dearest and one of them was nowhere near forty and one was quite generously past forty and the last was just kind of dragging some years behind you, and every time you wanted to say something serious about these eras you were exiting and entering you kept getting interrupted by the name Chana Morgenstern, because no one there knew whether she was a real person or a code name used by someone who was not in attendance and didn't like you anymore. So you let everybody else tell you about turning forty as the sauvignon blanc did its thing in the cooler bag and tasted amazingly of grapefruit. You would never be forty again, somebody had just brilliantly told you.

I began the day considering the possibility that the person I am before I set my eyes upon the page I'm about to read—in this case, page 79 of Herta Müller's *The Appointment*—is entirely different from the person I am once I commence reading. I know this because I am not Eastern European in my real life, at least I can't get anyone to think of me this way. I can't get anyone to understand how black people are another kind of Eastern European, especially not the Eastern Europeans. I can't get black people to want to be anything other than black people, which, as a black person, is incredibly inspiring, but on the other hand delays the thinking that black people are like Eastern Europeans, which could be of use when observing the state of things inside a book. But being "like," I realized as I somehow went on reading Müller, following her description of her narrator's most recent summons from a suspicious government official, is not the same as being "another kind of." How eventful it would be for the Eastern Europeans to begin calling themselves black, or even black Asian. How undermining of all that is the case were I to proclaim in my bios, "Renee Gladman is an Eastern-European African American."

I began the day trying to imagine a suitable place for an academic to attend a vacation; it had been a long time since I was a domestic tourist, and because it was only a long weekend over which I would travel, my destination needed to be in close proximity to where I lived. It turned out that I was already planning to be away, so I just did what I was planning to do, which was travel to Hilton Head Island, South Carolina, with my family, and by this I did not mean my husband and children, but rather my mother and two sisters. It was our first family trip in twenty-one years—it had taken that long for them to recover from the last time they vacationed with me. The scene, those twenty-one years ago, had not been pretty. It was an unfortunate period in my life where I seemed to have time only for Ayn Rand, a condition that left me sitting in the blazing sun for hours reading *The Fountainhead*, oblivious to all other forms of engagement. It wasn't just decided that we'd do this thing; we had to assess it as a family. After crunching the numbers—the years that had passed since that trip, the number of mood swings I'd had per day, now versus then, etc.—we determined that not only had I become far more companionable as a full-fledged woman-loving adult (V. thought my then-solemnity had had something to do with repressed sexuality), but also we discovered that somehow we'd all gotten old. So, we went and were all fat, or if not fat before we arrived, definitely fat upon our departure. Gwen, who'd been thirteen at the time of that long-ago trip, had now become everybody's captain. We did what she said do and only a short while after she said do it. I found that I liked to be bossed around in resort conditions: you can be sunning on the beach, drifting in and out of sleep, and at any moment the tall robust captain might stand over you and command you to do something. It was exhilarating to be told it was time to dress for lunch or that I needed to put away the Snickers. You might see how she was a government worker. However, the Snickers seemed to want to spend all their time with me. This was surprising, as we hadn't been close for years. But I ate them only when I was in the vicinity of the captain. She supplied the Snickers, and then at random times of the day tried to retrieve them from me. It was easy to eat so many Snickers that you put yourself to sleep as you stared out at the ocean from the oceanfront balcony. It was easy to fool yourself into believing you were eating Snickers when in fact you were eating rib eye and mashed potatoes. Soon I began to eat only these items and everything slowed—

my speaking voice, my bowels. It became a problem. No one could understand me. It was more than that my mouth was full. It was that I was no longer digesting my food. I couldn't get enough oxygen to form words. This was okay, in the end, because all I really wanted to say was, "How can Snickers be this good?" It was hot on the island.

I began the day reading the third section of Eileen Myles' *Inferno*. I was in "Heaven," and had been awake only a short time, still in bed, lying on my side. I hadn't yet had coffee, so after a line or so of the book my eyes would close. I'd be sleeping, except also reading. The book would go on in my mind as I slept (how much time passes in this state?), until suddenly I'd be awake and would find the book fallen to the floor (it wasn't a high bed) or sitting at an impossible angle in my hand. I'd right the book and try to find my place. The lines I'd been reading would not be there. Where had I gotten them? They continued the story perfectly, but not, it turned out, in the direction Eileen had wanted it to go. But, why? My additions were not terrible, and they seemed bodily connected to her text, and what's further, they stayed with me as I went on reading, mingling with the lines that actually were there. I woke up again. I was thinking this and not reading the page I was reading and I didn't quite know what I was thinking though it made sense with what had been on my mind before I'd fallen asleep. I'd been reflecting on how your mind writes what you read and lays it out only one or two steps ahead of you, so that there's always a risk of taking a step that isn't yet there.

I began the day in an audience lifting my feet from the floor one at a time, in recognition of something. I lifted the left foot. I lifted the right. I stared at him, the person onstage, whose actions were a kind of choreography: he used his arms and spoke loudly; he swung his arms. I stared at my feet and lifted them separately, now the right then the left, but brought them down softly. I was practicing, waiting, on my own backstage. There were patterns on the underside, debris from the previous night, but this wouldn't get in the way. Suddenly, the time had come. I raised both feet from the floor then brought them down hard, several times; then raised the one and the other in succession, slamming them to the ground, lifting, slamming. The speaker had finished, and we were doing all we could to make noise. You didn't want to use your hands; he'd taken care of that. I lifted my feet. They were dirty and tired, but no one seemed to care. It was an environment of relaxed standards: the main thing was to get the stomping of your feet to resound in your ears. It was also a place where when one person left the stage another quickly replaced him. It wasn't like church; you weren't in a fit. You did your work, then you were done, but you were a part of a string. It was hot outside, but inside we didn't fan ourselves; we weren't dressed in white. People were performing in a file. You banged your feet and someone took your picture.

I began the day looking at nothing move slowly in and out of focus on a movie screen. I stared at the expanse of it: I thought it was the night, I thought I saw telephone wires in the night, I thought I saw the bottom corner of the night curl up like a page. The screen becoming a kind of absolute for ten silent minutes, until the darkest part of the night became the top of a hill that took up the entire width of the lower part of the screen and the lighter part of what had been nothing suddenly filled with explosive shocks of light then it all went black again. Clearly, this new black was the nothing that I had mistaken the earlier black for. A person got up and went to the bathroom. I was writing in near complete darkness about this nothing when suddenly everything was repaired. There was an image of the sea. Though this surprised me, it seemed integral to this very slow-moving film. The sea moves but not in the direction of most things. I felt sure that most things moved from left to right or in the reverse. But the sea has an entirely other relationship to space; it seems to move backward, pushing at the end of it. The sea wanted to reach the end of space then to rush back here, then to push out, then to return again. It had been a long time of watching figures move across the screen on some type of boardwalk, moving in two streams in opposing directions; the light of their commute dull, and pink, and very dark.

I began the day in an embrace. Somebody was saying something; a car was crossing the earth on a highway. There was nothing but green fields, in a kind of architecture. The earth seemed proud of itself, which was part of the conversation I was having with the driver. She wanted to know if this was the letter or the essay I was writing, having promised her both. But the driver couldn't look at the passenger. And the passenger couldn't look at her lap for long (in her lap, she was writing). But she *could* look at the driver. The driver had to keep her eye on the road. It took a long time to fill up the page. I'd had to see that there was a small patch of yellow growing in a field as we drove along. And I was sucking on ginger and needed to swallow. You had a feeling that when you were turned away she had her eyes on you and wasn't driving properly. And wasn't driving. But neither were you pulled over. Would looking at her mouth bring on speech? Would it say what you wanted it to say as the car neared the hangar structure? Someone flung a door open in Denver, Colorado. "Someone jumped on my skin," I was writing when the question of the earth was raised —was it happy? She didn't think so.

I began the day in a fog that cleared before I'd gotten the chance to write about it. I was in one neighborhood, moving toward another, thinking, "This fog . . . ," but slowly such that it took me a while to realize I wanted to say more than *this fog* about it. I wanted to document it, talk about the glare it produced and what it did to my perception of the buildings of the city I was visiting. Eventually I thought, "This is an essay," then looked up to take it all in. I was surprised to see that the sky had cleared. It was a stunning blue and I had lost my memory entirely. That is not exactly true, as I remembered in vivid detail that I had just made a decision to look at the world (i.e., sky) in such a way as to produce an essay, but looking out at the world I couldn't figure out what was so special to say right then. It was a beautiful day in this place. I entered a density of streets that formed a plain, or maybe had a plain underneath. People were dressed oddly—high-waist pants, glasses with excessively large and hexagonal lenses, blouses and button-down shirts adorned in glitter and checks, patterned stockings with rips in them. Mostly, it was that everyone's hair was overgrown and flat or huge and beckoning. People looked frizzy, yet seemed to feel delectable. In any case, there was a feeling of elevation, like we were all riding glass-encased rising falling structures.

I began the day standing at a threshold of time—the beginning of something, the end of something. I had a method for standing that was called art, then writing. The way I stood allowed me to see how things could begin and end this way—simultaneously. It was hard to follow these opposing tendencies, especially when you were writing and couldn't see anyway, see anything other than these words appearing on the laptop screen. You were writing about something you weren't looking at. There had been a break. I was saying this on paper. I am not ready for school. I was typing this. Almost a summer had elapsed. I was looking at committee meetings ahead of me and *Friday Night Lights* behind. I was looking at the desires of my students. I was picturing January. I was picturing September 7. Aja seemed to be saying I wasn't feeding her. I was typing this. It was still summer. In a moment, Angela Rawlings declared her love for Iceland. I could see her threshold between her feet. Rachel Levitsky had a threshold. Martha had just crossed hers. Stacy kept changing her name. We were all trying to end something and were finding something new in the process, though what we found didn't seem to belong to us exclusively. Aja flew to the East Coast to go swimming, but there was a hurricane. Rather than fly back she sat solidly in the wind. I didn't hear from her for hours. I made cups of coffee. The day was tremendous. I wanted to name all the people who had threshold between their legs, and began to compile a list, which quickly became a volume, and was at volume 14 when it overflowed the walls of that writing.

I began the day waiting with my houseguest for a hurricane to ravage a city to the southwest, a city that was like the capital of the United States but wasn't. It was a situation of making coffee and watching the interactive map change depending on how intensely anxious we felt about the coming storm. I said "we" though I actually didn't know how to worry about weather. Many times I said, "We are frightened and obsessed about what's coming," but really I meant Aja was obsessed and frightened. Aja was headed to the coast and was hoping not to meet the hurricane, who had a girl's name. You couldn't understand all the calculations involved. It wasn't just that she would be on the coast but also that she would be at its tip, and didn't want to get blown out to sea, which does happen. Yet, she had flown all this way and there were many bottles of white wine that needed drinking. She wanted to run along the beach. The hurricane blew the famed city about then moved northward. Aja fled to the coast. I stayed here and wondered if I'd procured enough supplies. People kept running in and out of their homes with bags. I'd done this only once with only one bag. Aja was gone. The storm came. It was not wet as much as it was windy. I did not go outside that day. I ate my emergency supplies and stayed up late.

I began the day looking up at the whiteboard, wondering how I would do the thing I needed to do. My students were waiting. Robert Frost was their contemporary picture of poetry. I didn't think this would help them with Ed Roberson. I was going to try to draw a grid of light, as if one were looking down upon it, a grid that extended across an opaque surface, then draw, a good distance below that, a container, inside which were symbols. From the lower container, I wanted to draw lines that reached the opaque surface then became the actual lines of the grid. I would call those lines emanations. Without being essentialist, or perhaps being only momentarily so, I wanted to say, Often when reading poetry, it's the grid you're experiencing, and the grid is not the same thing as that subterranean container, where some meaning might lie, the actual story of the poem, rather it's the shape of the emanations refracted through language and feeling (though many contemporary poems have no feeling) that you're reading. I didn't know how to draw the effect of looking down on something, so I asked for a volunteer. Someone tall offered, and as I was looking up at his attempt to look down, I realized that there was a flaw to my thinking. The place from which the emanations arose was not intact, it was not a container wherein lay meaning. It was a grid itself but of what I could not explain within the allotted time. I had to let the class go: it was 3:51, one minute into their "free" time. I couldn't find my words; they remained sitting there. How could I send them off to read Roberson's book without having explained poetry to them. "There is a grid above and a grid below," I said slowly, trying not to uplift my voice into a question. Perhaps to read poetry was to read through a sieve. I wanted to incorporate the idea of a matrix. "Poetry comes out of nothing," I said, opening something I would never be able to close. 3:52. "Read the nothing," I shouted after them as they walked out the door.

I began the day looking into the infinity of the revision of my novel in progress. In fact, I had just exclaimed, "I'm afraid I'll have to start over," into a pre-dawn morning, when space expanded and I found myself in this infinitude. The novel, it was a wreck. I would have to begin again. I said this and looked at the screen for affirmation. "I have written sixty pages," I said, exasperated. "Houses of Ravicka, are you there?" It was hard to call the book out in this way, as it wasn't too long ago that I'd called the name of another book—asked it to step out of its hiding place, its refusal place, and come to me—and not only did that book never appear but I'd already written another book about its not appearing. I couldn't even call for *Houses* without it feeling like a rerun, and it was this—not being able to call its name but still looking at it, waiting for it—that gave shape to the infinitude, which was ultimately something beyond shape, which couldn't possibly have a shape and also be infinite. And yet, I clearly sat in a vastness (arguably a kind of shape), my pages blowing about, but never blowing about so much that I lost sight of them (they seemed to go no farther than the horizon: another shape). For months I ran after them, but pages floating so far away just begin to look like sky (infinity). "It's snowing over there, in infinity," I began to tell myself, and let that take the place of the novel for a long time. I was getting caught up in how a shape (my flailing novel) could be inside something infinite (not flailing), which would seem unable to contain anything (doesn't one need a body to hold?), but, perhaps in the summers, building pages all the same. I had sixty pages and a few ideas I wanted to share with the world, like geoscography, a science we all needed. But my novel was stuck in infinity, this snow system (sky), and was nearly untraceable (it wasn't clear how you could arrive there), and was itself looking for a shelf, some corner in which to grow old; although it was hard to find shelves and corners in absolute space, where geoscography made no difference (infinity being houseless). There wasn't a single house, a street, and nothing was needed other than the words *infinity* and *nowhere*. It made you tired to look into something without edges and empty of all the things it was full of. Eventually, I might encounter *Houses of Ravicka*, the revision, but could find many other millions of things as well, things other people were looking for, such as their own imponderable revisions or their own houses or songs. Could it be that every ten years you simply started something that couldn't be finished, that was impossible to finish because the person you needed to be to write the book never settled into form, or the form came and went while you were off teaching or buying furniture in a little city that stayed little the whole time you were there? I needed to say something about suspense, both in my novel and in my life, but in the novel you felt suspense yet had to plan it too, really removing any possibility for suspense when every second you were plotting it: why couldn't I discover it as the reader would and why, because I was writing this mystery novel, which had a real mystery—where was house no. 96, and was house no. 32, which wasn't there appropriately, actually not there in error?—why couldn't I experience the mystery firsthand? I didn't know where they were, either, why did I have to act as though I did?

I began the day recalling my bath of the previous night, which was scalding hot as usual and reaching the point where soon I would have to get out, or faint as I sweated through another page of Marilynne Robinson's *Housekeeping*. It was often when I was in the bathtub that my most cogent ideas struck me; yesterday was no different. When I reached the point where to read another sentence would probably have resulted in cardiac arrest, I laid the book down, and leaned back—this was the last phase of the nightly bath—and as I was doing this, there came an exciting new thought: if I was no longer going to write, as I had begun to worry that I wouldn't, then I should at least write about not-writing. And was so struck by the idea that I rose from the tub, dripping, to jot it down, which I was now doing. I was writing down the idea "I no longer wish to write" by writing down that I was writing it down. I wanted a threshold to open that also would be like a question, something that asked me about my living in such a way that I could finally understand it. I couldn't understand why my days unfolded the way they did and why they took me away from writing. I was writing, "I no longer wish to write," repeatedly, and in making this gesture uncovered distant, repeating scribbling from my child-hood: "I will not tell a lie," "I will not leave the top off the peanut butter," "I will never raise my voice." Each declaration filling tens of pages, and this was a kind of writing, similar to what I believed I'd been doing for some time—a writing so as not to write, so to find the limit (that last line) beyond which the body is free to roam outside once more.

I began the day thinking that writing was becoming a thing of the past as my fondness for Rollerblading now was, though in my time of writing and my time of Rollerblading—and these did sometimes overlap—I was far better at the former than the latter. I was far better at writing than I was at Rollerblading, and for the most part considered them vastly different. However, when they departed my life, they did so identically, robbing me of the ability—in retrospect—of remembering separately when I wrote and when I Rollerbladed. You were going to say that writing was for birds flying when suddenly a feeling came over you. Someone beautiful was talking about your sentences. It felt like rain. Things were starting to line up: history was speaking, which hardly ever happened to me. It was saying I had arrived at a moment where I could put writing down and walk away from it. I remembered the ache in my mouth when I ran into the back of that pickup truck. I was alone in a parking lot and had already given up too much—too much to brake, too much to swerve. I gave up most in my mouth, where a tooth chipped and I bit through my lip. I gave up most in going to the hospital. The language I had accumulated confused me, and slamming into the truck had cut my knees. I didn't know how to explain myself to the medic, but soon I began writing poems. In the ensuing years, the poems became prose, and I had written my last of it. Finally, I was done.

I began the day transcribing several of Gail Scott's sentences onto the wall of my living room. For months I had been trying to say something about them, which when I went to say it became layered, thus impossible as an utterance. I had already argued somewhere that one could not express many different things at the same time in the English sentence, and so was not terribly surprised by my failure. I'd learned that to think in this language you had to be patient: you had to say one part, like drawing one side of a cube, then say the next part, like drawing another side, and keep on saying and drawing until eventually you'd made a complex observation and a picture-feeling. You had to be okay that it took you twenty minutes to make this multilevel statement and accept that you hadn't actually scraped the surface yet of what you were really trying *to see* in this language. But when you were alone, when no one was there to listen to you unfold some puzzle in your mind, you coveted that ability to think in paragraphs with a single sentence, an ability you may never have had but that your instinct said belonged to you. I was saying "you," because I wanted to type this essay and draw on my walls in the same instant of 9:15 that

Sunday morning. In the center of the mural was the sentence: "Each time I start, it's as if the memory of the past (the noun, the sentence's beginning) wipes out the present (verb)." I wrote, "The woman sits still." "The woman sips her wine." I wrote, "In fact, this whole story might be more appropriate on a train." I wrote, "It's true, also, that in waiting, the space of melancholy can open up too much." I'd memorized these sentences years ago. I wrote, "Walking across this hotel terrace in the heat is like being in a postcard." I wrote, "Thinking that the problem with feeling better (calmer) is, it opens space for the inner anguish under." I wrote, "the inner anguish under" again, because it had reminded me of something. The mural was expanding and had now reached my dining area. As long as there were other rooms it seemed okay to rewrite those words until I understood what was particular about them. I wrote them as if they were a geometry instead of a verbal consequence. I saw that "the inner anguish under" was trying to tell me something about all the sentences I had just written, really reaching back to that first one. "Each time I start..." about progress through the sentence being wiped out by its own beginning, what the noun said. Suddenly, it became impossible for there to be verbs, or rather, it happened that the verb was in such a fragile state there could be nothing else around it.

There could be no duration. The "sentence" had to be divided infinitesimally. There was an "inner anguish" underneath. I resumed writing. I wrote, "Looking out window. Pale blue sky beyond anarchy of chimney pots." I lifted my wrist from the wall and rotated it to release the tension, then I wrote, "Below on sidewalk the pale man. Living in basement." I wrote, "Walking back down. Suddenly feeling happy. When old woman in thick black-and-white sweater. Asking help." I stopped. I breathed. I wrote, "For pushing heavy door open. No sooner falling over threshold with effort thereof." My heart hurt, I pulled my arm back, laid it across my chest. A few moments passed. I resumed, "When butch bouncer slamming it closed behind. Waving us down worn plush stairs. Entering red-and-white crescent-shaped room. Several lesbians dancing." My breath had grown jagged, and I couldn't repair it. These were the shortest sentences I'd ever seen; yet they were not the kind of sentences that allowed you to rest when you reached the end of them. They pointed always to the one up ahead. I was looking at the changing shape of the mural; what I'd thought was the effect of a strong sun in the middle room of my house was actually another kind of "inner anguish" in the language. You couldn't write these short sentences now without making paragraphs. Were you building the present?

The shadows said so. There were sentences that I didn't know by heart that were written in a notebook in the bedroom. I was worried about entering another reality, which would happen as soon as I left the drawing space. But the mural would not be complete without them, and would never be complete, but would be drastically incomplete without them. If I left the room now, the room with these paragraphs, I didn't know what I would find when I returned. Paragraphs had too much momentum to remain themselves. And really didn't hold content very well. But the walls were holding the paragraphs, and this looked likely to persist for at least the few moments I needed to run out of the room. I went and retrieved the last sentences. There was something dangerous about them. They pushed you off a balcony; they caused fissures in your reading mind. I wrote, "And day's final filtered trace abruptly snuffed by street lights. So railway-flat Room, indelible in middle, emitting air of stagnant or impregnable, into night beyond casement." I wrote, "The skinny deemed-dead-or-disappeared agoraphobe in window opposite." Then, "Old boats of once-amazing fries." I wrote, "That uncontrollable contingency, once more streaking past keyhole." Then wrote, "Whorling swarms + electrons." I wrote, "Acuiting." I wrote, "I/R surely kneeling on floor + placing fingers about your ivory throat." I wrote,

"Grandpa, in number of dreams lately." For a while, I hadn't actually been writing but doing a transcription that fell in the deep space between drawing and landscaping. I shaped, "As two clouds, in spreading, emitting low pink ray projecting full charge of light on Settler-Nun limestone or brick, an effect of cut-into-ribbons," and dropped the granite pencils to the floor. These were many of her sentences. I wanted to say more.

I began the day in a ceramics studio. I wasn't writing. I was decidedly not-writing; even as I held this pen in my hand, I swore I wouldn't write. I didn't. The ceramicist was beside herself. She couldn't remember her colors. Her glazing was out of control. "Was this Randy's Red," she was asking, "or Love Child?" Why hadn't I made a map, she wondered. She was a ceramicist with her creatures in her hands, wanting to glaze them, but the sculptor wanted the right color. I sat there. I was an unofficial go-between, yet neither the ceramicist nor sculptor required my services. It became hard to sit in a ceramics studio. Your arm began to hurt. You were doing nothing and there was this burning and swelling. Nests were accumulating. Only one of them said, "love Danielle." All of them had holes at the bottom. She was going to affix them to the gallery wall. Tomorrow, she was going to affix them. I had a hard time keeping track. I wasn't writing. I didn't take any notes. It was like nothing was happening but one person whispering and another gasping but not as part of a conversation and not in response to any apparent event. The sculptor was waiting for the ceramicist. Her arm was tired. A room of so many with no one writing. Night falling. Her arm reaching down, grabbing color.

I began the day with the profound realization that "the person in the world" was not a philosophical placeholder, as I had been treating it for the last twenty years, but was actually a student in my class of eleven silent girls. This sudden comprehension shone like a newly engraved plaque in my consciousness, though there remained no trace of how it had gotten here. I was stunned into involuntary meditation. I spent the morning on it. I am teaching "the person in the world," I weighed from a comfortable sitting position. Why aren't I flattered? I had to keep verifying: "the person in the world" was a student in my class of eleven girls and was one of the silent ones, which was all of them? Why hadn't she made herself known, or at least distinguished herself? How did one draw out the person who is the most perplexed of all persons? You couldn't be direct. You couldn't just say, "Will 'the person in the world' please stand up?" Or rather, "raise your hand," because you were still talking to that class of eleven shy girls. How did "the person in the world" end up in my class anyway? What was she doing at this institution? I wanted to know what her trajectory looked like. I mean, was she "the person in the world" *now*, or was she in training, in the way my students were training to be writers or executives of nonprofit organizations? It surprised me that "the person in the world" would be interested in writing. You'd think she'd confine her studies to anthropology or religion. What was she doing in a field that really left a person nowhere to go but further into herself? How would this help her plight as "the person in the world," who had suffered so much already?

I began the day wanting to read something about the Ravick-ians to an audience of Ravickian scholars or, at the very least, Ravickian enthusiasts, but I wanted to do this on a day that had the problem where most people hadn't yet heard of the Ravick-ians, much less their nation-state, Ravicka. I wanted to launch my small country into a world so crowded with countries that many hundreds went about in complete obscurity. Many coun-tries simply had no reputation at all. Yet they had people, lan-guage, and events as much as Switzerland had. And yet, some-how Switzerland had become famous and these many countries had not. I only wanted my country to be famous on people's bookshelves and for it to have geography. It did not need to be a member of the U.N.; it did not have to globalize its currency, it did not need others to invest in its debt. But it *did* want to be bordered on three sides and to look east into an enormous body of water. It wanted to be able to say hello to Latvia as it made its way home. I was saying "my country," but I didn't want one of those countries so small that someone actually owned it. Ravicka would not be incorporated. It wanted democracy but also socialization. It wanted governance without a name, something new that eked out of buildings. Ravicka wanted to be land first, then environments, then people. It wanted to be architecture then people. It wanted trees, architecture, people. Buildings first, then people.

I began the day looking into the cover of a book called *The Fold* for a sign and was not ashamed that this was most likely the same sign my students looked for when they approached the book *The Fold*, even though it was my job to have already found the sign and become acquainted with it, so acquainted that when I opened my mouth to introduce the book, a long trail of words would emerge and I would talk and talk, looking not into the cover of *The Fold*, rather into energized, comprehending faces, and we would go on in this manner—me talking, they imbibing of my talk—until not only was that particular class over but the semester as well: teaching became something that happened in a trance state, and semesters were one trance long. I was looking for the sign as the sun rose. Perhaps it was because of darkness that I couldn't see it. I stepped into the realm of metaphor, but it was a metaphor for reading rather than the one that would allow me to understand what I'd read. That is, the cover became a door—I could enter it if I wanted to. My thinking about reading advanced just that distance that allowed me to imagine opening the book and stepping into a room, now using my eyes to see in a way that I couldn't use my brain (although I knew these two organs were tandemic), but my understanding anything about *The Fold* other than "it should contain everything" remained stunted. I was reluctant to let the advance of my reading take precedence over my understanding what I'd read, so I refused the metaphor, though it stayed there as a question, wanting something from me. Since I'd rejected the idea of the book as a door, I thought now I can traverse the cover, by which I meant, "Now I can cross the street," which defied metaphor, because metaphor pre-empted motion. (In metaphor, the process of becoming was mercurial to the person encountering it [I never saw the cover *become* a door], I thought as I moved with my whole body around the room, and not just my thinking body but my world body, too.) Opening the book would be the first fold, and it was from this point that I wanted to speak. I thought it would be great to show my students how there was a fold at the entry of the book, and to walk through it was thus some kind of sublimation of "folding." Suppose the first sentence read something like, "You have just entered the fold of the book." I would recite that opening in class, then sit back and drink orange juice while my students thought about it. In fact, with that line I could go immediately to my trance state without having to say anything further, ever. You have just entered the fold of the book I wanted the book *The Fold* to say, but that was not what it said when finally I arrived there. That is the problem with reading other people's books called *The Fold* instead of your own, which you have not written. I needed to make a decision: would I go into this book and try to figure out what it was saying or would I project onto it what I wanted it to say? It occurred to me that if I couldn't read the actual book *The Fold*, then my students might struggle with it as well, and might choose to wait to read it until they saw my face, which meant I could do anything I wanted with the book *The Fold* and could even make it a mystery novel or a book about prose, pleats between sentences, the lip of a paragraph, the loose skin of reading.

I began the day wanting to fold the previous essay into this new one because I had learned just after writing it that it was possible to make beautiful, complex structures with paper and you did not need to be an architect to do this. In fact, I only needed one sheet of paper to achieve a beautiful structure, but it felt pertinent to this morning of my thinking that I use two. I was astonished to learn that you could build structures with one sheet of paper; I was even more astonished that you could do the same with two, and you did not need to go to school for this. I would not need to take engineering or design classes to print these pages and play with them, as the morning became night. I had to look into the mirror in order to take in these new facts. You could play with paper in such a way that you built things, and they were so sophisticated in form that you left them as centerpieces on your glass table. "These are my little ones," I thought I might grow to say. As morning became night, I forgot to get up and do anything that was not about folding paper. I forgot to go outside. I forgot to stand up and say hello to the ceramicist when she returned home. I forgot to ask the ceramicist to join me in my folding venture, because I was torn be-

tween being some kind of layman hero builder of paper struc-
tures and sharing the experience with someone who excelled
around paper, who said things like "The hand is a book" and
typed to candlelight and held votives over dictionaries. Some-
one yesterday said, "And we won't know what has departed,"
and I thought this was true about people who began building
architectures out of paper on which were typed many words,
some by candlelight and some by the ordinary glow from a
bulb. You won't know who's entered the house with seedpods
gathered from the street and whom you missed saying hello to
and who is now running along the dark streets for exercise.

I began the day sitting in a kind of isosceles to the ceramicist, who at that time was not a ceramicist but a person sitting at a desk with etymology. She wanted to walk into a word and then into another word and another and keep walking until her comfort shoes turned into boots with tassels and her hair swung and her hips did a kind of dance. It was wrong to say that she was not a ceramicist; rather, she was not working with clay at the time that we formed this awkward triangle, with our desks and my desk lamp and her microscope. She was a ceramicist all the time that she handled pages and made strange noises in her part of the triangle. She didn't call my name. It was all of a morning. But we sat like she was the road that returned drivers to the city and I was the road that sent them to the countryside. I sat like I was chief of a newspaper office and she was a cartographer. She was closer to the door. She was closer to the closet. She was closer to the bookshelf. Everything about her situation was city. I was country, because all I had was a wall, the one behind me, the one to my right. The ceramicist cleared her throat, but it wasn't about me. She wasn't trying to have a conversation. She didn't want to know what I was writing. She turned the page of her book and changed the angle of her foot. I wanted to know more about the shape that held us; it was perfect to the room. All the books were silent. The candles made us feel that somewhere there was an oven. The light was sweet and had a little song attached to it.

I began the day connected by several moving points on a grid, in a constellation of live objects, in a house of memory. My body was a container for the conversations occurring on the floors above and below me, the messages being left on my phone, and the letter I held in my hand. I was a shape but one where everything inside me was in motion and I was trying to hold it mathematically, trying to be a pattern in the world. I woke lying beside something that was geometric but also a poem. One of the hands on my belly didn't belong to me. The poem had extraordinary cheekbones and liked to talk about Emma Kunz drawings. Sometimes the poem got up early for work and erected a border of pillows around me, intended to hold me in place. The points of the grid had words attached to them, words arranged in a row of six to ten groups, and had spaces where I could stop and see that I and everything inside this grid were moving, as was the grid itself.

I began the day seeing something pass from one form of life into another. It was a grandmother leaving. I didn't see it happen but was saying that I wanted to see it. People kept saying she had passed, and I felt myself turned toward some light in the sky. I found myself having turned, but was not present in the turning. I found myself with a memory of having turned but wasn't aware of my body turning, or of any data it may have gathered in the process. I didn't see the light. I only had a memory that I'd seen it. I was looking at this memory, which was nested among other memories from that moment of my living. However, neither this memory nor any of the others seemed to actually exist in the world. They were not this desk where I sat, where I leaned into an artificial light and it was three thirty in the morning. The light I saw when someone mentioned this passing was a memory: it sat in me. It was not part of the world. I could not pick it up, yet it caught my attention. It had become a story of something that had happened to me instead of something else I wanted to happen: what I'd wanted was to see this passing. I didn't understand how a story could just end. Someone said something that made someone else's story end and made my body turn, and made me vacate my body while it was doing this but left me with an imprint of its duration. Someone only had to say there was this passing for that to be the end of fiction, at least for the moment of the body turning to see the passing as some visual occurrence at the back of the head, something evinced by looking into the sky, rather than the real passing of one energy form into another.

I began the day in a room with Antonioni's *Red Desert* and thirteen students, some sprawling on the floor, some sitting in desk chairs as I was, and we were moving toward a horizon that only I knew about, because the rest of those in attendance had not yet seen Antonioni's *Red Desert* and didn't know what was coming to them or what would open. We were looking for a poetics of space but I had to keep getting up to adjust the volume. We were looking for architecture in everything. But, I couldn't get it loud enough. The subtitles were clear but the voices were soft and the clanking of machinery soft, which didn't make sense for an Italy of 1964. Soon I got the sound right and the noise lifted the hair off my head and off the head of Jennifer Avery, who sat on the floor in front of me. The clanking machines were beautiful; the movie let us see them. For an extended moment, the movie showed us men gazing at the beautiful machines (though these were working men, not students and a teacher); the men were gazing at the machines and we gazed from a space behind them. We saw against an overcast sky enormous iron structures spitting steam the same color as the sky into the sky so that you saw it and then it was gone yet still there, which was clear because the movie and the men went on looking at it. There was a lot of gazing in the film, people frozen in space, gazing at the strung-out land or at other people: for example, Monica Vitti's gazing at a small crowd of her friends, husband, and possible lover. We find her in a standoff in the fog; it is a frozen moment. She wants to run (as Giuliana, deserted) to the car then run the car into the sea. But the crowd blocks the way, except there is fog, which is more powerful than these friends of hers laid out like rocks across her path, and it engulfs them and makes them disappear, long enough for Monica to run to the car (as Giuliana, deserted) and drive the car nearly over the dock edge. She stops short though, as she would go on doing for the rest of the film, completing nothing, which was one part of what Antonioni wanted to ask in this film— something like, What do we do with our inertia?—the other part being color. To ask about color the walls needed to match the women's sweaters and if you were wearing a gray sweater you stood over against the white wall and if you were wearing a red sweater you stood against the blue wall. "Such that the whole film gave off architectures of color," we were saying that next week in class. Such that there was this "intimate immensity" that hummed through that evacuated landscape and sent Monica Vitti (as Giuliana, deserted) from one empty scene to another, in the dark, alone, except for the red of an abandoned train, except for the Turkish man who shows up.

I began the day having to vote Yes or No to support the decision that there would be no decision right now but that there might possibly be one in two years' time, excepting the case that there isn't. I sat with the voting slip in my hand; we were to come down on either side of the situation, but the situation wasn't clear: "Am I voting to support the failure to make a decision or the decision to have failed?" I tried to find where I was: "I mean, am I voting to support the committee who reports to have failed to make a decision or voting to support the decision of the committee to have failed?" They answered that I was supporting the failure, its failing, and the committee "at large." It may have been simply that what we needed no longer existed such that we had to stop looking for it, or we had to call it by a different name, or we had to change the posture of our looking, or the very nature of looking had somehow become a problem for our eyes, or we would rather just go on as we were and invite a friend over occasionally. I wanted to begin drinking wine. "It's now or never," someone murmured from the screen hanging on the wall. "It's not now and not never," someone corrected.

I began the day thinking about the university level—where it was and who was allowed to go there—and felt in my body a sense that there were a series of gates to pass through, a grand lawn, a series of gates and then an elevator to take you down into the earth. The university level would be on the top floor of something that rose above all the surrounding structures but did so, inversely, deep beneath the ground, perhaps forty levels below, where meaning was made and the core burned brightly. You had to take a bus to reach the site where the university soared, and it took seventeen days and six months, and the rules dictated that you go alone and read nothing and sip a little bourbon. To go you had to take a bus and climb into the car awaiting you—any person with a map and credentials could do this: going and getting on a bus that arrived and departed from eighty-two terminals before pulling into the lot where a hybrid car awaited, a car driven by a person with a book in his hand, the only book you would find on your journey. It was the car that drove through the gate and ran out of gas two times, one time overnight, and provided a place to sleep: the driver standing outside. And dinner coming on a tray that bore a map of the place you'd been earlier that day and something in you growing very tired the more you ate. I could see the landscape from where I sat, writing about the landscape. I was on campus. I was at the university level, but I couldn't remember how I'd arrived there. I had to watch people for years to put the story together. You took a bus that drove all day for many days, then climbed into a car; the car eventually drove through gates—one gate and then another and stopped for lunch and then four more gates—until it pulled up to a building that looked like an enormous well. It was brick and wood and cloaked in mist. You had long forgotten about the sun. The well had a door that the body had to squeeze through and a thick rope that the body scaled down; at the end of the room the body landed in an elevator. A picture of a book was pasted next to the controls: it was maybe your book, your first, or a book by your favorite author. There was a sign that talked about the university, how you might find it, which button to push. But it didn't explain why the button wasn't on the panel, the button for the university level. You ran out of numbers before you got to where you were going, so just had to sit there. You sat, I was told. And nothing happened. No food came; no one screamed down to say hello. You waited, perhaps for days, perhaps in a timeless way, and suddenly felt a jolt. It was a different feeling from the bus, which jolted, but horizontally. This was a free fall. The body fell in a cage through darkness, sweating and inhaling the core of the earth. The core called out to you in a torpid voice.

I began the day wandering the streets of the small city where I lived in pursuit of two variables—acts and location—that belonged to the same expression—*acts of location*—but mysteriously so. I was looking for an event (in the world) that would index the moment the expression came into being, such that when one said "acts of location" sound or sight would confirm it. Moreover—I thought as I meandered—the event needed to occur between my body and the city. That is, I wanted to express, within the object world, a series of acts of location that needed only the body (and the world) in that moment of expression. Yet I also wanted to find the variables of the expression as independent facts in the world and, between them, to recognize some form of visible scarring that would indicate not only that I'd found those facts but their interrelation as well. The scarring would act like a body (though not mine), which one approached with a word that functioned like a name but didn't have to be the name that necessarily belonged to that body but could be a name that the body put on for a time then took off to hand back to one. It needed to be a name that could be worn by most bodies, because the idea was that you'd find scarring everywhere, between every gesture and the space that manifested around it. I was trying to see location the way I saw wind blowing the small branches of city trees. I tried to have it sync up with the incessant sparrowing I heard. I wanted location to be ordinary and for acts to be countable. However, I did not want "acts" to be sitting on top of "location" in such a way that you were metaphysically indisposed, having to pull the two apart as I was now doing. There had to be a pre-space, before the expression, where they were adjoined but not merged. An act was everything and location was everywhere, which made the whole thing hard to break down, but when you said "acts of location," you didn't think all possible things at once. Rather, you narrowed in on a feeling, a specific event that made a boundary in time. I was trying to walk through the city with this unfolding. I began northeasterly with pieces of paper on which I'd scribbled the words *draw* and *bird* and *call someone*, and carried those pieces to sites I thought of as "church," "bus station," and "art gallery," leaving each piece in some kind of correspondence. I laid *draw* within "church" and pulled out my recorder. I hid *bird* behind a trash barrel at the "bus station," then got on a bus. Somebody asked me what I was doing when I began making new slips for "acts" on the bus. I tore the paper with ceremony and hunkered down to make the folds. A person tried to grab one, but I retained it at the same time that I put *call someone* in his pocket. I thought he might fall to the floor and allow his face to open. I thought he might do something devotional. But instead, he stared and did not blink. You couldn't understand it if you couldn't ask about it and you couldn't ask about it unless you revealed the act in his pocket. I walked into the "art gallery." The ceramicist had her nests on the wall. They already had pieces of paper coming out of them, so there was no place to put my words. I still had "acts" to pass out. I had *fold*. I wanted *fold* to be an act of location and I wanted everybody to have a nook. Inside the nook, I felt, we could understand something that had always eluded us. We would know enclosure. But, that would be "place," and place was not precisely location. I let the thought go. I grabbed a hand, then came another idea about acts, how acts are sometimes like pocket notes that you use to process an experience or work of art, how you might hang nests on a wall and nest in each of them fragments of a manuscript and let pieces of that book fall to the floor, such that within that sequence would be seven acts and seven pocket notes. However, though "the floor" could be argued as location, a fragment falling to it was not the "acts of location" we were looking for. The ceramicist wanted tequila before her opening. We didn't know if going next door to drink it was making new location or just extending the old. We didn't know when our tequilas stopped belonging to the name on the bottle from which they were poured and became parts of the "bird" we uttered during our sips. There were always extra folds of birds of paper and you could move your finger along the length of them and have witnesses, and do this for minutes at a time never having to explain what you were doing or the desired effect, because it was clear that these folds were the scarring that made people feel safe in public.

I began the day wanting these essays to do more than they were currently doing and even had a book alongside that I thought would help me, but it turned out I wanted more from this book as well. It was hard to be a book about engineering in architecture when an essayist wanted you to be a book about structures in fiction. But why were you called *Atlas of Novel Tectonics*, if I was not supposed to think of you this way? Somehow I'd wandered into the middle of a letter. I signed off and returned to the day, a cooler, dryer morning than the one before. I sat in a gaze of wanting more as I drank coffee and looked into these essays for their architecture, waiting for the sun to rise and sleep to come over me (fictionally). Not only was this book's title *Atlas of Novel Tectonics* but also it had the title "Geometry" for its first section, "Matter" for its second, and "The World" for its final! What should a book on novel tectonics concern itself with other than the nature of fiction, a fiction trying to amass itself and become a huge structure? Fiction was trying to amass itself all over the room where I sat, but a morning rain had begun (fictionally) and I was trying to write an essay. I was between fiction and essay and flipping through this book that called itself an atlas, that had microchapters that made my heart rush. I wanted to enter the space of "refrain" (tucked inside "Matter") and think about recurrence in an unfolding novel: (Ah!) I stretched back and leaned into the rain. I didn't know what the book on fiction architectures would say about refrain but this wasn't that book, which meant that book still hadn't been written and I certainly couldn't write that book today.

I began the day trying to understand how the phrase *slam dunk* functioned when uttered by the president of the university at which I was employed, who was, in that moment, explaining how I would soon be dis-employed from that university and pulling from her gallery of expressions the phrase *slam dunk* to drive the point home. The reasons for my dismissal were cloaked in a mysterious mystery (as if we were in a double tunnel), and I was trying to find a clearing. But she'd said "slam dunk" then relayed a story about her life, which, I believed, was intended to place us face-to-face in a rolled-up-sleeves kind of way, where she could say, "slam dunk," and I could lower my head with humility. I thought she might have been writing fiction, because the whole air of why I was there was that she knew more about fiction than I did, as did the provost and some other men at the university level, so "slam dunk," which she confessed I was not, was an opening to some novel she was writing. "Were you a slam dunk," a passage in the novel read, "it would be easier for me to see you and to listen to you, but I am tall and the wind is blowing through my hair. In fact, only something loud, something that would crash down on this glass, that would replicate one hand emphatically putting the situation into a clearly defined hole such that there was no possibility of mistaking anywhere and in any light that (a) there was a ball and (b) a hand that delivered it and (c) something gained from the ball delivered—with violence—through a hole that stood alone and had arrows pointing the way . . ." And so the president's novel continued beyond the point of our meeting, into the cycle of my sleep, clanging through my dreams.

I began the day with the president's novel in my hand. I was surprised that it was a slim novel not unlike those I'd written myself and I was torn between reading it right there (at the university level) or waiting until I was on the toilet, where all short, delectable novels should be read, or at least begun. However, I couldn't commence with the reading of the book, which, I believed, was the president's first novel, which, surely, would win some huge prize in no time—I couldn't commence with the reading of this novel until I'd read the one—written only recently by the provost—which absolutely influenced this one I held in my hand. But it was hard to find the provost's novel, because he wrote it in such a way that only a select gathering of men could read it; in fact, one could never be certain—since you were always hearing the story at three or four removes—whether the provost's novel was actually written by the provost or, on the contrary, which wouldn't actually be that contrary, was written by that small gathering of men. It was hard to find authorship among this group, and yet one knew, one could not deny, that this center represented the future of novel writing. I liked that I could hold the president's novel between my thumb and forefinger without putting any stress on my wrist. Her novel was as light as a rag, and I appreciated this when I had to slip it out of my campus box, as if it were made of explosive materials, because even though it was a compact novel and I have always appreciated things that were in miniature, things that were hazy in content and direction, especially novels, this particular novel I felt would be to my detriment, and if, as I was retrieving it from my box, it touched anything else it would harm that thing as well. But you wanted to read this novel, because it was written by the president of the university for which you taught, or by the provost or by that small gathering of men. In any case, it was written by a mind that knew everything there was to know about fiction and understood "impact" without having to understand anything else.

I began the day just trying to get a handle on their sexual entanglements: everyone had been with everyone and was now with someone else in the room. Everyone had tried love or sex with one of the people sitting here, then later on tried love or sex with another of the people. They had been men and women doing this, and if I were to get up and go, they would be alone. Though the way they loved or had sex would probably not express itself immediately: I didn't think if I left the room they would begin tonguing each other or fighting or writing each other into their books, not that day, not in the middle of a meeting nobody wanted to have. As I sat in the room, I wondered about all the people who were outside of the room, who also could be added to this map of loving or sexing, who were not here because they didn't belong to this institution yet belonged to this network of lovers. Sometimes through these negotiations you realize your purpose: they needed me. I was the only one who could get up and leave, and if I did leave, it would only be to bring the others back with me. I had a quest, and it was in service of my colleagues, but it was not the kind of service valued by the university, so I was torn as to whether I should do it. It was hard to fathom the consequences. If I brought all the people who had loved or sexed all the other people in this room, where each person had loved or sexed at least two of the original people present, and they were all together with the stories of their past relations, sometimes written in books, sometimes forgotten, and I sat among them having slept with none and having read none of the books, what would I do while they were reminiscing and what would I do?

I began the day wanting the language to describe a kind of writing that one could do that was not a physical act of producing marks on a page or computer screen but was a duration of thinking in which the thing one had recently completed, in my case *Ana Patova Crosses a Bridge*, which moved through my life so fast, so crisply that I couldn't find in my body any feeling of having written it—I found the memory with no problem but nothing in my muscles or in my breath that could tell me something of what it was like to have written that book . . . I wanted a duration in which the book I had written, which was the third in a series of books, a book in which fatigue made me break the line before it had reached the requisite length for a novel—it was a novel, but one tired of the form . . . I thought perhaps the reason I struggled to remember in my body this book that flashed through me was because immediately upon finishing it I went straight into drawing, though it was drawing that was rather like writing, and maybe there, in the drawings, was the record of this book I had made. I made the drawings because I wanted to inhabit a thinking space, one that could be seen and was not just a story we imagined about how thinking went on in our heads. Now I would be able to point to an aggregation of marks and say, "Narrative is like this," or say, "These are the mechanics of prose." At the time, though, I didn't want to say too much about the drawings; I was interested in the silence of writing. Nevertheless, I must have had in me some memory of what it was like to build that book, as it had become one of my favorites of the books I'd written, and I had written it listening to someone listen to me as I shaped it. I regretted not having been more aware when I was writing that book that I was writing something I would come to love, that I would eventually put next to another book, written many years prior, and call the two my favorites, and actually admit this to other people. For me to have known this was happening, I needed to go back in time to that day in January, the day before the book entered me, and say to my body that what was about to happen would be important, not only because a manuscript would emerge from me, cellularly, and would go out into the world, as the third "trying" of something mysterious and essential to my living, but also because the way that I would have to think in order to write the book would change me from that point forward, and later I would want to look back on the stages of that transformation and see the inscription of this new thinking. As I had done before, I would make the way the book changed me a book in itself, or at least make an essay that would draw a picture of the story.

I began the day trying to explain to Danielle what it was like to be a lesbian in the 90s and why there were so many ex-girl-friends around who were often in committed relationships with other ex-girlfriends of yours as well as one or two others in the room, these others also being ex-girlfriends of other friends there, not friends you ever slept with but friends between whom floated some strange tension, residual of something that happened fifteen years ago, which no one remembers but which everyone holds vigil. And how one of these people might sud-denly grill peaches with mint, causing us all to gather around the table. And how one of these people now has a daughter and another daughter and son and two dogs named Jesse and James and how they all might gather at the table too, eating those peaches. I wanted Danielle to want to be at this table, though she didn't know any of these people previously and had grown up with better boundaries in another part of the country. She missed this decade where we just couldn't burn our bridges, where we built bridges on top of ruined bridges, and lived in an elaborate architecture of trying and failing to try then at the last minute trying, escorting some broken love into what looked like a better love, until that love broke and that old love became an even older love who moved on, perhaps to someone you roomed with or someone a person you roomed with once loved. We didn't know what it looked like and wouldn't have called it community, but now there were all these people and they liked the grilled peaches and shared the pork ribs elegantly. It was that the peaches were basted with a balsamic reduction that a person had prepared on the stove, a person who was now in love with my best friend's ex-lover, my best friend who was once an old love, but is now my friend Chubby who has Kristy and kids. Chubby wasn't there but wanted to be remembered and placed fondly in the center of any photos that were taken and was happy to be a cardboard cutout in these photos: she was happy to get a smear of the peaches, even just a whiff of the ribs. Danielle didn't eat the ribs but did eat and eat the peaches and went on for days thinking about them, wanting to recreate them later for a different gathering of people that comprised no ex-girlfriends and no friends of ex-girlfriends, so was not as warm as the previous gathering and the guests were not as old. They didn't remember the 90s in the way I did and didn't have fourteen bridges built over one piece of water and didn't have water.

I began the day hearing the voice try to take on layers and speak about poetry and speak about prose and be a loose figure that people wanted to write about but no one wanted to be. The voice had all these responsibilities, but everyone was forgetting about it at the same time. You could write a poem that was the repurposing of another poem—a text that was perhaps found in a catalogue for farming equipment, that you lifted up and placed on a new page with your name on it—you could use tractors to show your thinking and wouldn't have to say "I" and wouldn't have to say "please" about anything. You wouldn't say, "Please can I write the story of this light bisecting the room, where a person walks in and stands, not knowing what to do." You'd just say something like, "Tractors la la la, thousands of dollars," and write your name. Maybe erase it then rewrite it. Maybe change the typeface of your name. Make the font small. Add shadow to the third and sixth letters. You might write "Mr. So-and-So" instead of your name. But the voice was getting away from us. First it was everything and then it was nothing, though it was the same language we were using. We stopped talking about the poem as though someone were inside it, then we stopped talking about the poem altogether, or at least stopped expecting there to be a body relating to the poem, at risk. It seemed possible to say anything, especially if someone had said it before, and it was these words of that other person that we put in place of our voice. People were doing this then saying the word *internet* after and waiting to hear a response. The response came: people had lunch; they found language everywhere. The menu said "Fries," and this was taken, put on a page next to "Omaha," punctuated by a date. We wanted to map instead of talk; we wanted to silence something and open something. There was so much detritus building up: it needed to be written; it needed to be used. Someone wanted to laugh at it. If you could find a space to laugh, then that voice inside you—the one that went "Please, can I"—that voice might lean back and read the newspaper. Time would go by, and structures would be laid on your name.

I began the day "a woman in clothes" wanting to be a woman in clothes, because Danielle had had a certain body all her life. And I had had a certain body, but where she had regained the body of her life, which she had temporarily lost, such that she carried a memory of the other body but didn't have to see it, I had this body, which had been mine for a long time, but which may not have been my body, in that sense of Danielle's—a body she liked to drape in clothes. My body was wearing the red pajamas and hers the dark green and hers made a shape around her butt with a line bisecting, and the line wrote "ass" all over everything. My line wrote "penis-pocket," because of the slit, the pouch at the front of the red pajamas. And the day was getting on. I was wondering how to be a woman in my red pajamas and thick red wool sweater, my skintight pajamas, my striped sweater. I was wondering how, if the bell rang, I would run down the stairs *a woman in clothes*, as if someone had written a story about our day, where we stayed on this side of the snow that was falling, and the inside was our city. We wanted a city full of living, so we walked quickly back and forth in front of the full-length mirror. She swished past me; I swished past her, with hours passing. We were women in clothes for a time (despite my undershirt being tucked into my skintights) and this made you want to get to know a person. "You are red everything," she said, looking all the way to my socks. But, my slit, my pocket made me shy and I was dizzy from the speed of my walking: I was in my skintight pajamas and carried, in them, a voluptuous body that was probably an impostor. My sweater sat on top of my belly; my socks slid across the floor. I was red-black-red-red-black in that order and something else in reverse. Then several hours passed. "She was now in a white shirt," wrote the story, "a blouse, intersected by blue infinitely. And, though the woman was dressed ..." it carried on. And though Danielle was now in bed—I began writing my own story—she was wearing jeans, and this was her body. To find mine, I had to push my hand through the slit of the red pajamas, and show the ring on my middle finger: it was something along the road to getting there; it was a feminine gesture—if you looked only at the grace of the hand—an accessory.

I began the day trying to say the word *body* as many times as I could, for myself and for everyone in this room. We were in a time where the body was important to a lot of people, and it was important to me. I wanted to exchange the word with all my correspondents. I wanted to say "body" to them: how is your body or writing through the body or how the body activates objects in the room. I hoped to say "body" and see a change come over your face: inside your body, the edge of the body, your body split. (I split you.) I hoped to reach a point in speaking where when it was time to say "body" I could go silent instead. I'd pause and everyone in the room would sound the word within themselves. I'd go, "Every time you put a hole in the _____," and demur. Lower my head like a forty-watt bulb, look solemn. Or would say, "We all carry something in our _____" (it could also be plural), and the collective internal silent hum would overwhelm my senses. This would be real communication: something you started in your _____ would finish in mine.

I began the day obliged to clean the moka pot, which I had failed to attend to last night, but I cleaned the fry pan instead. I cleaned the fry pan and sang loudly a Valerie June song and remembered the moka pot then further my first cup of coffee, which I hadn't yet had. I washed the plates from dinner; I ran the garbage disposal. I sliced into a lemon and placed a quarter of it into the sink. I took a deep breath and felt something alight in my chest. It was a small fire that might have been a clog beginning to form in my aorta. I thought, "I will never take a hot bath again," as I proclaimed every morning. I had been sitting on the kitchen floor with my hand clasped to my chest, in proximity to the moka pot not-quite-gleaming on the stovetop, the closest I'd been to it in hours, and I saw in my predicament a reflection of the problem I'd stumbled upon the previous night. The problem was in the form of a question: In order to draw (was how it began), would one have to give up writing if to keep on writing one needed to draw—writing and drawing being identical gestures made with the hand—would to stop writing so as to draw make drawing impossible, since drawing was a way to think with the body and writing was the story of the body in thought?

I began the day inside the world trying to look at it, but it was lying on my face, making it hard to see. The world was made up of layers, one encompassing the other, and it smelled like onion. I didn't want to think that the world was an onion and that, in order to describe this world, I would have to describe the attributes of an onion, which had been done many times already. But, I couldn't deny what I was smelling, nor could I deny that seeing myself inside an onion or belonging to an onion (perhaps not quite located within it, locatable) provided a useful way to observe how I was a part of something that formed a sphere of folds, where one fold lay organically next to another, each one thicker as you moved outward, away from the core, though onions have no true core, or, rather, no core that survives our trying to reach it. And that was why I thought it was difficult to understand this world. You dislodged the thing you were trying to find, and whenever you moved, it moved. It balanced your moving by moving. Who wouldn't be happy to live in such a world? I was happy, but if I were going to think about this world in addition to simply moving about in its folds, then I'd have to find a position from which I could do this effectively. I tried out all the levels. I could never tell if

I were in time. You needed perspective to study geography. You needed an "I" to understand "we." It was impossible. I began to think there was no real evidence I was living. We all believed we were in this multiplex, though there was no way of proving it. The books said you were in a world: they told you how to accumulate worldly things; they said if you looked to your left there would be an object; they told you what you were sitting on. Suddenly, there were names that went for things that were and were not there. Sometimes, there was a chair or a train, but sometimes there was not. It depended on things bound by a logic that existed outside the onion or, if in the onion, always on a layer other than the one you were then on. I wanted the world I was part of to be the kind of entity I could verify, and to verify your world you needed to be able to bend down and pick anything up. It couldn't sometimes be there and sometimes not be.

2.

I made a shape by placing a figure inside a word and pushing the word off the page, so that in my mind and in the mind of anyone reading that page, anyone who knew the language in which I was writing, a picture of living would emerge that had a time and a place and objects different from the world of the body writing or reading that page, and this picture could play and pause at will; although not separate from the body writing in that familiar world, where a cup of tea was growing cold. The picture was dependent on the body but, unlike the world in which the body typed, the picture could play and pause and could itself be divided into further pictures. I sat down with the objective of pushing words off the page and bringing a picture into being and doing this for a number of hours in a row, for a number of days, all accumulating into a number of months, perhaps amounting to years, such that this became a picture in which was embedded many other pictures and that gave off a dimensional feeling, even though these pictures belonged to my thinking and were nestled in my mind, which like everything else in thought was not like a pot you could pour water into and heat up but rather was like seeing a pot and having a living vision of all the actions therein. You made a space that gathered all the possible pictures accreted through all the pushing of words off the page, and many times called the shape *novel* and a few times *essay*. I set the cup down. I pushed the words *I set the cup down* off the page, then picked up the cup and set it down. I drank from the cup, though I didn't remember this until I'd read the act on the page, my reading having become a picture of a body standing at a window with cars parking below. But it wasn't long that I was in this body thinking about the cup at my mouth or other things the body needed when I realized that all the cars parking were doing so all at the same time, and this was strange. It never happened this way. You never had a moment where every car on one street was parking at once; you never had a street where all the cars had been gone then returned all at once, all wanting to park and all finding a space to park and parking at the same time as all the others. Wherever it was that I was standing provided me a vantage point in which the information that I gathered was becoming a problem for the picture that held me. I had to grab another picture and append it to this one, so that I didn't get stuck, perpetually sipping from that cup and looking over cars behaving bizarrely.

3.

One of my favorite words was in my mouth, and I was torn between chewing and swallowing it, so that it could become a part of me, another organ that processed or eliminated some material of my being, or spitting it out immediately, without doing any damage to its form, so that I could study the word in all its glory. That word was *sentence*, and it wasn't just that I had the word *sentence* in my mouth but the essence of sentence as well, such that against my tongue I felt that I was harboring a kind of chain, as one might wear around one's neck, but rather than being made of metal it was paper in content, though nothing like the paper one wrote on or drew on, perhaps more like the paper one glued and immersed in water and turned into sculpture. My sentence had sculptural content that I couldn't deny. I began the day with this word in my mouth that absorbed every other word around it. It sucked everything in and enforced an order that made me particularly aware of time. I tried to move forward in my mouth, using this paper chain to describe the experience of being in my mouth. I was ready for its philosophy; but when something is in the mouth, there is not always that clear relationship of container to contained. The thing inside you could be so enormous (in concept) or conversely so minutely intricate (like overlapping web structures) that although your body encloses it, *it* is the only reason you know your body. *It* is the only way you have to say, "There is something in my mouth." Something reversed on me when I tasted *sentence*, as if now I was consumed, sealed inside some container; and though this sounded like a bad situation to find oneself in—mouth full of papier-mâché, a word that represented all thought structure sitting right on the tongue—it was like dreaming inside a machine, or dreaming up a machine that was your life.

4.

Every day of my life I sat in a room and this was akin to writing: I sat and stared and wrote without lifting my hand, without turning my head, and stared into the humming of the room I sometimes called "prose" and sometimes called "San Francisco." That city was one of the places I'd been and simultaneously was one of the things I did while I was there. I did the place I was in, because the place was entirely itself, so to be there was to do it, and this was not something that happened everywhere you went, and rarely was doing a city the same as doing prose, as was the case here, and even more rare was the memory of that doing becoming the room you were in. I was in the room of San Francisco when it occurred to me to write, and write all my life. The room was separated from the rest of the house by a hallway; there was a hallway and at the end of it a place to go sit and write. I did every kind of walk down this corridor to arrive at the room of writing, and I walked with every kind of feeling, so that it wouldn't always be the same text I was writing. But sometimes it was the same until later when it wasn't. The rooms in the house of writing had names like "white room" and "mud room" and "where we sleep" and "the table," and these were the stations the hand moved through while the body sat still and never moved, remembering a long-ago city, which both ceased to exist and went on existing in your typing, being dispersed, spread out between words. I wrote in San Francisco then stood up and shut the door. With the door shut, I closed the window, creating an airless space for description. I closed the window and made a spread of the pages of the book I was writing. It was the driest the room had ever been, and this dryness, this airless space without a hint of moisture, changed my thinking about what I was doing. I stopped thinking about typing and poured ink over the surface of these pages then took a small stick and drew circles and wrote my name then let my name dissolve in the ink and wrote my question on top of it. I kept writing and letting the script dissolve—one utterance on top of the last—now writing backward, now making *sense* only in my mind as I let my hand do whatever it wanted (it wanted to write but no longer in the language to which it was accustomed) and still on that spread of pages where I'd poured ink and drawn circles. From the circles, I drew squares that looked like houses, though none of these houses bore any resemblance to the house

I was in or to any other houses that populated that city. This made me want to write a novel, a novel that would tell a story about drawing in San Francisco an architecture that existed somewhere else, beyond the frame, and the novel would be in the midst of unfolding when I'd have to stop writing to draw— but not those houses that I'd been writing about, rather the sentences that conveyed them.

5.

I sat in front of it and felt distinctly without conflict that we were separate: I was a body and it was an object, albeit the most thin I'd ever seen and the most cavernous. I was a body and it was a page and we both had our proverbial blankness. I was poised to write. I was poised to open and write or to open and let writing happen. Since it had yet to be determined what writing actually was, how it formed, and where it went once it was made, you didn't know what you had to do in order to write. You seemed to want to make a map of that blank slate; you seemed to want to make a mark; you seemed to want to pull a mark out of the blankness. The page opened. It was clean but it crackled like something was living there. I wondered about the signs we were wearing—if somewhere on me was the sign "writer" and somewhere on it was "page," because somehow we knew what we were going to do. I was going to make a mark and it was going to open and crackle and seem electrified: blank but full of presences or questions. My blankness was harder to define; when I looked for it—reached into myself for it—it was only the page that I found. But I didn't know whether at some point in my past, perhaps at the very first moment I set out to write, the page had fallen out of me or I had risen out of it.

6.

I was trying to write about having drawn on a morning that was held in fog; I wanted to write about the drawings I'd done and I wanted to talk about how I'd arrived there through writing: I looked at the drawings. There were hundreds of them. They were numbered, so I read their numbers out loud. I was trying to put the drawings into a line without touching the drawings, which were now back in their box: you couldn't touch the drawings for very long, because they were fragile and liked to absorb things from the object world. My drawings liked dust and fingerprints and sugar from dates. My drawings had names like *PA 210* and *PA 04* and they lay in harmony in the archive box. But somewhere in the object world I'd decided I would talk about the drawings: I'd give them language so that I could say they weren't language exactly. They were underneath, something appearing out of something being exposed, and I wanted to say it was language with its skin peeled back, but you couldn't use peeled-back language to tell an audience that the drawings were language peeled back. You had to use language with its cover and point away from language to show how language could go around exposed. Language was beautiful exposed; it was like a live wire set loose, a hot wire, burning, leaving trace. If you looked into language this way, you saw where it burned, the map it made. The wire was a line, but because it was electrified it wouldn't lie still: it thrashed, it burned, it curled and uncurled around itself. It was a line but one that moved, sometimes forward, but mostly up then back then over itself then out then up then curling in one place until the mark grew dark then out forward and up into a rectangle then inside the rectangle and around, circling with small, tight movements. I was amazed that I was talking about wires when really I was talking about prose. I was talking about how it was to write, but doing it through drawings (but drawings were language) and using wires to spell it out, but I was doing this on a foggy morning, where there were neither drawings nor wires. There was a table, upon which sat a computer, and I was staring at a screen imagining the drawings I had made and wanting them to teach me how to talk about the line, the line in art, which I could use to talk about the line in language, because you'd need to know they were the same line. There was not a thing different about them. They entered blank space and made a problem for the page—what next, where to go—and they were lovely in themselves. I buried lines of language in the drawings, but the lines weren't trying to say anything definitive. It was usually a question they wanted to ask, but not one I felt like enumerating in that morning, where hours had gone by—one hour—and the fog had remained. With this city you never knew whether there would be fog all day or just in those first moments of the morning. I wanted to expose something about the fog, so I sat down in language, language that had never seen fog, which was the problem I was having. I wanted to write about something of which I had no understanding. I didn't understand lines, and couldn't tell whether anyone else did. I read about lines in art and couldn't understand why they wouldn't talk about language. Monika Grzymala said, "Drawing is a process of thought which is conducted by the hand," and she was an artist, and though she was using language to explain her art, it was her art that most concerned her. Drawing was a process of thought—that was true, and so, and especially, was writing. And we wrote through the hand, even if it was typing: we used our body to write. "Thus, drawing is writing," was how I wanted the quote to go on. And to write was to think; to make lines was to draw; and lines were the essence of writing. I made a line, and though it couldn't be read, the narrative of my line began instantly. I made a line; it couldn't be read, but I felt the story in my body. It was as experimental as everything else. I made the line while talking in my head, which was what I did while I wrote. So I was writing, but it was drawing that had accumulated.

7.

You would drink something and it would bring you back to the long table at which you sat and the writing that needed to be done, the writing that would be the beginning of forming a new line between writing and drawing that extended into a story of writing and drawing then became a drawing of writing and drawing and then a novel taking the same terms and asking them to build a room or a series of rooms or a series of fields in which the sheer fact of one's wandering could bring one upon a moment in which drawing and writing were intertwined, encountered as one gesture moving across space and making the body want to sit down and respond in some correlating way—correlating because it would be a conversation that never ended, always begun and staggered and begun, rupturing, never completing itself, rather, endlessly repeating, starting again and again, in the sense that sometimes beginnings are slow and last forever and everything you need is within them.

8.

I wrote and considered another espresso on a day so hot sweat poured down my back, and even this made a line between writing and drawing—another line that would require articulation, itself articulating—you were sweating down your back when again the idea came to write, to write about what has happened outside of writing but having everything to do with writing. I got up and left the café only to return two days later submitting my body to the same conditions—the sun bearing down upon me, dividing the field of my work into an upper and lower landscape, two parcels lying side by side. The parcels were important and differed from each other in a way that would be revealed through writing. I was sweating and couldn't think any longer but liked to go to this place to sit and drink coffee and grow very, very hot. It was too hot to write but these landscapes were forming around words that were on my pages and on the pages of a few of the books I had with me. One of the books was an autobiography written as a theoretical essay, as a book of fragments about what one had read and eaten and seen in various parts of the world, the photos one had taken; and after moving across all these pages you arrived to the last where sat a word, wholly different from any other word in the book. It was a departure that seemed to want to go from the word as a signifier to the word as an entity made of fibers that could be drawn out across the page until that word could no longer be read but was still enough like a word that you tried to read it anyway. This act formed the upper land-shape. There was another word in another book that couldn't be translated but which brought to mind a place in the back of another place. This formed the lower land-shape, and recalled to me something Rosmarie Waldrop said (misremembering her translation of Edmond Jabès): "the book at the back of the book," where all this writing was heading and where the day already was. You were in a field, an unidentified country, and all the lines were illuminated and lifted out of the ground.

9.

I made the same drawing every day for 433 days and gave each a number. I tried to number the drawings according to order of creation, and mostly achieved this. I made the drawing—I drew—and then I turned the page. I lifted the page; I turned it back, over the place it had just been—no, it was more *behind* that place. I lifted the completed drawing and I turned it back, with care. I placed it behind itself. That is not right. I lifted, I turned: the drawing lay not over the place it just was but behind it. But, not beneath the subsequent drawing. I would finish the new drawing and lift it up to find the old drawing. Rather I would turn that new drawing over such that it lay on top of the old, as long as I was drawing. As long as I was drawing, each new drawing lay lightly to the left of the one it succeeded. It was like laying folds of cloth; I laid them down, but this wouldn't be how I would wear them and place them in closets. The drawings were not alive yet they lay on top of one another: I treated them gingerly. I drew. I laid the drawings. They were stacked, made to lie one on top of the other. They were oldest closest to the front then younger as you moved deeper into the pad I was then using. Because I had this pad, I did not need to number the drawings immediately. I lifted one up. It seemed done. I was happy with it: it was a day like any other where I sat to draw and drew because this was my new way of writing and wrote because this was the only way I could draw, drawing seeming crucial now to my thinking. I wrote to think: I lifted, I turned. I made adjacent spaces. And for a long time I didn't number them. Numbering seemed to indicate that something was done. You put a number on it and placed it in a box, and let a stack grow. You looked into the box as if for illuminated texts and found these drawings. These were the drawings you drew. That's what you were trying to say. "I was drawing these drawings, finishing them, giving each a number then placing it in a box, and I looked at the box lovingly." I loved the box. But, it wasn't something that I talked about immediately, to anyone, because drawing was embarrassing. I was not writing. I was drawing. Yet I was drawing writing so I was writing, but at the beginning I didn't know how to say this. I wrote a calamity. I wrote another calamity. Sometimes they made me sad because I thought when I finished them I would be done with writing.

I thought I am writing myself out of writing by writing, and not because my taste for it was diminishing, nor because I was losing content. I was losing writing because I had suddenly begun saying what I needed to say, but it was because of drawing that this was happening.

10.

Sometimes the drawings were ugly because what I'd done was take the concept of the cross-out, magnify it by ten and remove it from context such that there was no cause for elision, no evidence of a relation to the elided, just cross-outs. But it wasn't just cross-outs going across the page because those would have been grid lines and would have been beautiful and made you think of Agnes Martin. No, it wasn't just cross-outs but something swirling underneath like broken dances being written about in cursive language broken already in the hand before the hand wrote, so needing to be appended. First, you started swirling in brown ink as if to write the thing you were thinking, the thing you'd recently placed between something you wrote and something you did—it seemed like swirling in ink might at least bring its character to the fore—but it was hard to know before you began swirling, before you put brush to paper, whether this would be the swirl—the thickness, the right stroke —that you needed to say what you were going to say. I used the whole plane to lay down this language in walnut ink, which seemed to die once it hit the paper, once it dried and became rust-colored and dead and thirty years behind you. So I added those cross-outs but I made them in black; they were like a fence I built directly over my own head, across an afternoon, watching the sun move across the sky. I made slates of black, thinking I could get the line to talk to the swirl, to pick the swirl up and take it somewhere it couldn't go by itself. I waited for it to dry. I waited. I waited for it to dry, then I stopped waiting. It was something you wished to complete but couldn't because of the problem and the sense of urgency that if this problem went on existing, even for one moment longer, it would make all future drawing impossible. I couldn't have this mess on the page, this dull color lying on top of this dead one, so I added white to the not-dry black and something gray and snake-skinned was born. It was as if I were trying to paint, building layers, creating a textured mound that anyone would want to stay away from, not touch, not glean.

II.

I wrote into the days, not drawing. I wrote not drawing and
this was surprising to me. It was the first time in a long time
that I wrote without drawing as I was doing now, as I was still
doing. I would recognize myself not-drawing and would won-
der what it meant, what this material was and did it have con-
tent. I had grown used to content being the gesture I made, the
curving line, the box that was always sure to appear, the loop
that came later on. These had become my words, my sentences,
and I'd become so familiar with them that I didn't have to talk
to myself any longer when I was doing the writing that was in
fact drawing. When I was doing the writing that was also
drawing I didn't feel lonely the way I sometimes felt when I
was only writing. I liked to see the lines coming out of my
hands; I liked to see where they would go. I drew against a hum
in my head that was like happiness. The line came out of the
hum most of the time and landed in the space of the page, be-
coming buildings, becoming paragraphs, being a suggestion of
urban planning, being a suggestion of energy, how energy be-

haves in space. Soon, it was less a hum that led to drawing than it was a particular attention (the opposite of humming, more like dreaming); it was an intense attention that moved and stopped and circled and stalled, then made a line and went up and down and was a box, which usually necessitated another box in proximity. I was drawing something I had seen somewhere, something I had felt as I walked among buildings and perhaps something Eva Hesse had done, Maria Helena Vieira da Silva had done. I did this writing-drawing again and again, for days, for months; it became my work. And was now the way I went about writing, rather than this version I was later doing. Yet, it would be incorrect to say only *I was writing* when clearly this was a writing that also drew. It was not as much drawing when my fingers were doing this with keys, when they were typing, but you could argue I was drawing because that's what I was writing about, and you could experience the nostalgia of this exchange: writing about something you weren't doing because you were writing about it. But, I couldn't just draw and not tell the story of my drawing. I began to tell the story of my writing-drawing and I told it many times, and it was the same story again and again. I never grew tired of it: I kept writing to say I was drawing and somehow this was drawing, too. I wrote, "I am writing drawing," and felt so satisfied, so finished in my growing as a person. You finished growing when you began to write what you were doing; you suddenly think you have reached the end. So, I was reaching the end of writing and was writing the end of writing (because you want this story told as well), but then I truly did stop drawing. A whole day went by. I didn't draw, and what I'd drawn the day before could not bring me back to drawing, because those drawings were not successful. They were in-between drawings, asking questions about drawing but not loud enough to be heard. I had made a life where I was saying "drawing, drawing" all the time and writing it, expecting people to notice but not get upset. Please don't get bored that I keep saying *drawing*, I thought as I wrote and drew and wrote about drawing and drew writing until the day I stopped to exclusively write, to say goodbye, to say I am done. I have done all I needed to do. I stopped to write and what happened was that it emptied me. I forgot everything. I forgot that I drew and that I wrote to draw and so didn't know why I was writing. It was a different kind of stopping.

12.

It was often that the act of drawing produced two effects: a drawing and a paragraph or so of writing. And though at times I argued that these were one and the same—a drawing was also a paragraph of writing—in this case you would have a drawing in one hand and a written text in the other, making two texts combined: one written and one drawn. I was afraid that when I finished the book I would only be able to write that I had drawn; I would never again see in that writing drawing itself or see when I was writing that it was a drawing I'd made. I feared I would not be able to say "drawing" again and again within the smallest space of writing, where you could only go six or seven words before again you had to say the word *drawing*. I understood that this was a special thing that was happening to me; it was a gift and it was my work. I was thinking it, making it out of blood and gas and whatever else is in the body, but I was also tapping into something that had been there long before me. We didn't know how thinking existed in time, what time in thought was. I didn't know whether it was "today" in my thinking as it was in my sitting where I was writing this: at a desk covered in books and pencils, a desk whose shape was a letter. Language was everywhere, and it had time, but language was not thought, or rather thought was not solely bound up in language. You could draw to think; you could trace your hand along that wall, build something. If I ended the book here, would the thinking that had guided me this whole way cease to show itself? Would it just lie down and grow quiet? I wasn't ready to stop saying "drawing" and seeing how drawing was made out of writing, but I couldn't go on in that form just saying "drawing, drawing"—not developing the word, just loving how it changed what I was seeing through my saying it.

13.

"The Eleven Calamities" were now twelve in number and had become something quite different from earlier parts of the book, but belonged in the book all the same, and more so each time I tried to get out of the book, which was every time I wrote last month and these first days into the new month. I didn't want to leave without saying what I needed to say, but I couldn't put into language what it was. I could only feel it. What I wanted was for what I said to amount to "This is what I was seeing" but to do it in a way that what I said brought forth the thing I *saw*, rather than a representation of that thing. My words would reconstitute the thing I'd seen exactly as I'd seen it and create for the person reading those words a verisimilitude that enabled her to believe she'd also seen the thing and in that initial moment that I'd seen it. You wanted to write a whole book, where people were just seeing how you lived, and you did this for a long time. But then your living became a way of writing, and the events you wrote about, which were non-events in the crucial way that this was why you were writing of them in the first place—for much of the day nothing happens, nothing ever happens, you were trying to say—these events became structures for thinking: so you were walking and drinking coffee or not drinking coffee and your pattern of thought was changing. My sentences had changed somewhere between coffee and drawing, and then I was writing to try to catch up with the change but all the time making more change because to write was always to add to something that is going its own way. You can never describe what is there, only what you see, so that what is there—if this is something you want to hold on to as well—gets its own language, somewhere underneath or throughout yours. I had the drawings and multiplied them through writing then drew more of the drawings because of the writing then began to love writing about the drawings so wrote more about them then drew more. "Sometimes I put the drawings aside," I seemed bent on saying. "Sometimes I drew myself out of writing." "Sometimes I drew when I should have been writing and this made me think I had reached the end of it finally, writing." I kept writing that I was no longer writing, but then also looking at the drawings: shouldn't they be better if they were now all I had? I had to write in order to figure out what I wanted from the drawings. And I had to write in the drawings *as if drawing* because this helped me formulate what I wanted to ask: At what point? At what point did my sentences become this way?

14.

I began to write the last of it without knowing, without saying anything about what I was doing to anyone who was around, which was one or two scientists in the rooms neighboring mine, and a musician and a scientist farther down the hall, and an artist and a scientist down the other hall, and a fiction writer, and it was Friday, so no one was around to see the end of things or to hear all this language winding down or to think simply that because I was here, sitting how I was (with my door ajar and their passing back and forth, perhaps to the printer, perhaps to find coffee), that I was finishing something, finishing but also trying to get swept along a line of thought that would be so long and strange and profound that I could follow it for days and days, not only aging as this happened but also growing joyous and carefree. I wanted to write into a new territory, for "the book at the back of the book" to be a country that was both unique and livable, not a country where buildings came up and surprised you but where existed rooted buildings with lines that were linguistic in nature, lines emerging in such a way as to change language, to bring you down to the street. It was amazing to see a line move from one mode of being to another mode nearly counterposed to the first, as when concrete becomes paper, as when something that is rigid, performing stability, collapses into a curving body at the floor of a page, without scenes of the building itself collapsing—making death and chaos—but the mind just moving from the first context to the second, following the line. The line wanted to thread everything I was saying and wanted to talk above me. I was louder but I had to keep turning to the line for emphasis: I couldn't make my point without it. We were staring at a blank space for as long as we could because my point began there. I said, "Encounter." I said, "Threshold." I had read "ecology of experience" in a book. The page was a "commotional field," I had read. I was saying that the blank space was already commotional when I turned to look at the line, which wasn't yet there but which was a vibratory presence in the room. And it wasn't just one line that I felt but every possible line, pressing at every possible opening in the field. The field was commotional: it did not allow stasis. To enter it, you had to be in motion, and to see where you were you had to be in motion, and not just moving your body around constantly, frantically naming stations, then moving at varying speeds between them, but also naming with impermanence, seeing objects as in the middle of some process, and understanding your seeing as impermanent as well, changing always. Once I'd done this, I could look at the line falling from the building and speak differently about it. I wouldn't have to say one then two but could create a relation that sat outside of one and two, something that can't be named here in this space of one and two but perhaps could be pointed to. I was trying to say how so much was going on in the space of the unsayable, when we were looking at that blank page, when I released the first mark across it. There was everything that happened between the line and the page—your being able to say, I have just made a mark; it is a beginning and so on—then there is all of the activity that occurs from the feeling of your body bisected, your eyes bisected, the time in which you were sitting, there is the fact that space has changed, that history has been opened (this line came from the past). "It opens," and I said "it" entirely without knowing to what it referred. We sometimes say it when we don't know or when we have gotten lost syntactically. I was not lost but I was trying to get in between. This was an essay in which you were allowed to pursue the unsayable, even though the pursuit perpetually returned you to the beginning, your first mark, the moment before anything could be said: "It opens," I had written into the space of the space to feel the onrush, the invisible matter, what math tries to account for. "It opens, and many people throw up their hands" is a problem you insert into space. Yet this was what I was saying rather than my pointing to what was unsaid. How did I lift this cover? I asked, and that was when the line fell to the floor. A doodle that does not end is what? It was an ephemeral gesture made in the margins that I hoped would go unseen; it was a line searching for the book at the back of. "It opens, and many people throw up their hands in the causeway." Something kept growing: my hand moved outward (it wanted a letter), it moved out and into a shape that looked like an *e* but was not an *e* because of what the next shape was. It was un-al-phabetic, it was a small loop—something returning something to someone; and when it completed itself it made an extended straight line, not coming out of its center but from below as if to underline a figure that wasn't there (not yet there). You didn't know if you were always waiting for something to arrive when you were writing or if you were, conversely, following something. I said "something" because it could be anything and could exist outside language: it could be the unsayable, that invisible matter that was brightly lit in certain situations. You didn't know what time wanted to do to you. You didn't know where time stood in terms of direction. Was progressing along a line of language moving forward in time? It didn't seem so, since I was still trying to say what I wanted to say, an idea that occurred to me many moments ago, that was now no longer with me but had hold of me nonetheless. I wanted to get to the brightly lit situations, but they seemed out of time. It seemed one needed to write in order to see; one had to move out across the page and then through—but maybe not *through* the page. It would be movement nonetheless and would require the body to transform, the physical body becoming astral or like a line itself, moving further in. Something. But how did you get out of language from language? Is the book at the back of the book actually in the book? There was an elsewhere bearing down on me, in the whiteness of this space. We were staring at its blankness, and this was when I lifted my arm and brought my hand close to the surface. I made a mark: I moved my hand slightly to the right and ended on an upward curve. What would come next would be a continuation of that gesture, but at what level I couldn't say right then. I couldn't know where I would go next without first going there—that is, when doing the kind of markmaking I was doing. The itinerary came from something beyond what I could sense, and it barely existed. It came out of nothing, some place so microscopic it could not exist in the present of my searching for it: it seemed as if it was one point and the place I was going was another point, partly because I could see my hand travel in its effort to arrive there, but I was reluctant to conclude that when one wrote one wrote as one from one. We were staring at something blank and I needed to interrupt the space. I wanted to show you something about articulation and memory and time. I wanted to ask you about things, how they came into appearance, how that thought erupted from your mouth. What would you write as I wrote? To put something in that space was to make a field of a field that was already there, and it wasn't so much that the day was getting on as that I couldn't talk about the line falling to the floor without picking it up somehow. And would have to do it in the past, where soon it would be too dark to see.

ACKNOWLEDGMENTS

Earlier drafts of some of the calamities appeared previously online at *Triple Canopy*, *Floor*, and *a Perimeter*, and in print in the following journals and anthologies: *Stonecutter*, *Open Letter* (a special issue on Gail Scott), *No*, *Dear*, *Women in Clothes*, *Broome Street Review*, *Paris Review*, and *Best American Experimental Writing 2015*. Many thanks to the editors and readers of these publications.

Additionally, a broadside of the "Nothing moving on a movie screen" calamity was printed by Mills College's graduate letterpress program, and was written for the filmmaker Kabir Mohanty.

Quoted phrases from the "Gail Scott's sentences" calamity were bibliomanced from the following Scott novels: *Heroine* (Coach House, 1987), *Main Brides* (Coach House, 1993), *My Paris* (Dalkey Archive, 2003), and *The Obituary* (Coach House, 2010).

Immense thanks to Wave Books and, especially, to my editor Heidi Broadhead for her steady and attentive presence throughout this process.

Many of the essays in "The Eleven Calamities" section of the book were written during a yearlong fellowship at the Radcliffe Institute at Harvard University. I extend my deepest gratitude to that community of brilliant, elastic minds from disciplines across the sciences, humanities, social sciences, and creative arts. It was a live engagement that restored me to my senses.

And lastly to the figures, ghosts, friends, and heart-ones who cross the pages of this book: I call your name.